Spelling Rules and Memory Tricks for A
To learn & improve KS2 spelling and voc

British Years 3 and 4 — KS2

by
Joanne Rudling
from www.howtospell.co.uk

Do you want to learn some secrets and tricks
to help your spelling?

Spelling Rules and Memory Tricks for Ages 8-9:
To learn & improve KS2 spelling and vocabulary

ISBN: 9781080884971 (paperback)

Published by
How to Spell Publishing
www.howtospell.co.uk

Contents

Spelling improves if you:
- ➔ study it
- ➔ practise it
- ➔ think about it
- ➔ notice it
- ➔ write it

Be a spelling detective and investigate peculiar spellings.

Key Words — Statutory Words to Learn

Here are some of the spellings you need to learn in Years 3 and 4. Some are easy and some are really tricky, so we'll take a look at how to remember them. We'll also look at how to change them with prefixes, suffixes and rules.

accident(ally) — 8, 16, 50, 52-56, 59

actual(ly) — 50, 52, 53

address — 7, 16, 65

appear/disappear — 7, 15, 40, 45, 47

arrive — 47-49

believe — 7, 9, 10, 14, 45-49

bicycle — 17

breathe — 49

build — 10, 39, 40, 45-47

business — 13-15, 65

calendar — 7, 9, 16

caught — 23, 24, 28-31

centre — 9, 49

certain — 40, 50

circle — 49

complete — 9, 40, 47-49, 51, 69, 81

continue — 40, 45-47, 53, 70, 83

consider — 70-72

decide — 9, 46-49, 68, 75, 76, 81

describe — 9, 49

different — 9, 17, 56

exercise — 9, 49

experience — 9, 40, 47, 49

experiment — 9, 52, 53

extreme — 7, 9, 51, 56

famous — 47, 49, 82, 85

favourite — 16

February — 8

grammar — 7, 9

heart — 7, 16

heard — 15, 24, 28-32, 35

imagine — 49, 70

important — 44, 50, 56

increase — 41, 49

interest — 9

island — 16

learn — 15, 26

medicine — 9, 17

mention — 69, 75

natural — 9, 41, 45, 49, 53

notice — 47

occasion(ally) — 50, 52, 53, 76, 78

opposite — 7, 9, 15, 49, 69

ordinary — 52

particular — 57, 59

peculiar — 14, 15, 58

popular — 40, 57

position — 9, 15, 71, 74, 81

possess(ion) — 65, 68, 76, 78

possible — 39, 42, 51

potatoes — 9

pressure — 17, 49

probably — 50, 51, 53

promise — 49

purpose — 17

quarter — 56

question — 69, 74

recent — 9, 50

regular — 39, 41-43, 47, 57

reign — 24, 28-31, 33

remember — 7, 9

sentence — 9

separate 7, 9, 14, 49, 51, 70

suppose — 17, 49

surprise — 49

therefore — 9

thought — 10, 51

through — 24, 28-31, 36

special — 56

strange — 51

various — 82, 85

weight — 24, 28-32

Introduction

Welcome to the wonderful world of spelling.

This book is full of **spelling tricks**, **rules** and **fun tips** to help you understand, learn and love spelling.

➔ If you feel like this about spelling, working through this book will make you feel like this.

Spelling is stupid!

➔ Have you got your coloured pens and pencils ready?

➔ A spare piece of paper is good for trying out the writing exercises.

➔ Don't race through this book — take your time and enjoy it.

➔ Enjoy the words, art, writing and exercises.

➔ And remember, making mistakes is good if you learn from them, so don't get stressed about getting things wrong.

➔ If you don't want to write in this book, grab your favourite notebook and do all the exercises, writing, word art and drawings in it.

Word Study

You have to work on spelling and study it just like maths, science, history, or any other subject.

Spelling a word correctly happens when you **get to know a word** and become **friends with it**. Ways to do this include:

✓ knowing how it can change with **spelling rules**

✓ understanding how we can make it longer with **prefixes** and **suffixes**

✓ noticing the common **letter patterns** (also called letter strings)

✓ using **memory tricks** to help you spell it if it's a tricky word

→ In the **Word Study** sections, we'll look at the **key words** you need to learn. We'll discover: the rules, letter patterns, vowels and consonants. We'll use memory tricks, as well as doing *word art.* Then we'll write sentences and draw pictures.

Top tip: → **Use a dictionary if you don't understand a word.**

Using Memory Tricks to Remember Your Spelling

Do you want to know a secret?

You can use all sorts of **tricks** and **strategies** to **learn** and **remember** your **spelling**. For example, you can:

✓ See **words within words** (*piece of pie, add an address, my heart is in art*).

✓ See **vowels** (*remember, extreme, excellent, grammar, separate, opposite*).

✓ Notice the **root words**, **prefixes** and suffixes (*unusually, disappearing, unbelievable*).

✓ Use **syllable breakdown** ("im-por-tant", "ex-pe-ri-ment", "Feb-ru-a-ry", "Wed-nes-day").

✓ Spell with **rhymes** and **sentences** ("i before e except after a long c", *never believe a lie*).

✓ Use memory tricks to help you spell tricky words.

✓ Know **spelling rules** (drop the 'e' — believe ➔ believing).

Good spellers use these strategies and memory tricks all the time, especially to remember difficult spellings. You might think some are fantastic, or some are stupid, but that's fine. Use what you like and what works for you.

➔ Using memory tricks, **seeing words within words**, and **noticing vowels** are important methods because sometimes we forget spellings when we don't use them all the time, especially tricky spellings like *calendar, believe, address, separate*.

➔ To help us figure out if it's *calander* or *calendar, adress* or *address, seperate* or *separate*, we can use some of the strategies above. We'll go into more detail about these in the book.

Top tip: ➔ If you come up with your own **memory trick**, you'll remember it.
   Use whatever works for you to help you remember a spelling, no matter how crazy it is.

Word Art and Drawing Pictures

➜ *Word art* and drawing pictures help you remember spellings.

➜ Adding details to the letters — shading, doodling around the letters, or colouring in the vowels or difficult bits — can help you learn spellings.

It's *brrrr* in February.

➜ Your pictures & word art don't have to be perfect; just enjoy putting them down on paper.

➜ Do some WORD ART for your name.

Spotting Vowels

➔ Spotting vowels is a great strategy, especially for dyslexics.

Look at these words from the 2019 SAT spelling test: excellent, division, deceive. Noticing the vowels could help with the spelling of these: **excellent, division, deceive.**

This is just one of many useful spelling strategies to help you. If you love it, or find it helpful, then please use it. You can use it in combination with the other strategies we're going to look at.

Use colours to highlight the vowels.   Look at these **key words:**

remember, recent, sentence, therefore, extreme, centre
believe, experience, experiment, exercise, complete, different
grammar, calendar, natural, separate, interest
decide, describe, medicine
opposite, position, potato/potatoes
difficult

➔ **Do some word art for these words and use colours for the vowels.**

➔ Sometimes, the meaning of a word can give us a clue to the vowel letter patterns:

beech or beach?

A b<u>ee</u>ch is a tr<u>ee</u>. / A b<u>ea</u>ch is by the s<u>ea</u>.

➔ Use memory tricks for difficult vowel patterns: Colour in the tricky vowels:

because — Because you need to **a**lways **u**nderstand.   bec**a** **u**se

build — **You** and **I** b**ui**ld a house.   b**ui** ld

believe — Do you bel**ie**ve **I** exist?   bel **i** **e** ve

thought — **I** th**ou**ght **o**f you.   th**o** **u**ght

Exercise

1. Can you guess these key words without the vowels?
2. Now add the vowels.
3. Check on opposite page to see if you're right.

r e m e mb e r,   r e c e nt,   s e nt e nc e,   c o ntr e,   e xtr e m e

gr a mm a r,   d e c e d e,   c a l e nd a r,   o pp o s i te

d i ff i c u lt,   d i ff e r e nt,   th e r e for e,   i nt e r e st

n a t u r a l,   s e p a r a t e,   m e d i c i n e,   e xp e r i e nc e

Bec a u se you need to a lways u nderstand.   I th o u ght o f yo u.

Do you bel i e ve I e xist?   Yo u and I b u i ld a house.

10

Answers

remember, recent, sentence, centre, extreme,
grammar, decide, calendar, opposite,
difficult, different, therefore, interest,
natural, separate, medicine, experience.

Because you need to **always** understand.   I **thought** of you.
Do you be**lie**ve **I** exist? **You** and **I** b**ui**ld a house.

1. Rewrite these again in your notebook and use the *Look, Say, Cover, Write, Check* method.
2. Rewrite them again using different colours for the different vowels.
3. Get your friend or parent to give you a spelling test with these. Or record them and test yourself.

➜ A words-within-words preparation exercise

Warning! Multiple choice exercises can really mess with your brain because they give you spelling alternatives which also look right!

Multiple choice exercises are only useful when you can use various tricks and strategies to help you, such as:

- using memory tricks
- understanding spelling rules
- knowing common letter patterns
- seeing vowels (We've just looked at this strategy.)

We'll look at these in more detail in the book.

➜Look at these important words (key words from the curriculum word list) you have to learn to spell. Which ones do you think are correct?

➜**Don't worry about making mistakes. Mistakes are fabulous** because you can learn from them, so be bold and choose the one you think is right — no stress because this is between you and me.

| 1. a. seperate | 4. a. beleive | 7. a. peculier |
| b. separate | b. believe | b. peculiar |

| 2. a. favarite | 5. a. calender | 8. a. presure |
| b. favourite | b. calendar | b. pressure |

| 3. a. different | 6. a. business | |
| b. differant | b. buisness | |

Answers   ➜ *Look, say, cover, write* the words and then *check* them carefully.

1. a. ~~seperate~~
   b. separate   _____, _____, _____

2. a. ~~favorite~~
   b. favourite   _____, _____, _____

3. a. different
   b. ~~differant~~   _____, _____, _____

4. a. ~~beleive~~
   b. believe   _____, _____, _____

5. a. ~~calender~~
   b. calendar   _____, _____, _____

6. a. business
   b. ~~buisness~~   _____, _____, _____

7. a. ~~peculier~~
   b. peculiar   _____, _____, _____

8. ~~presure~~
   b. pressure   _____, _____, _____

Remember, don't worry about making mistakes. In this book, you're going to learn how to spell these tricky spellings and then use them in the writing sections.

➜ I know multiple choice exercises aren't as hard as spelling the words in a spelling test or writing, so that's why it's important to practise these words in the writing sections in this book. Or get your friend or parent to do a spelling test with you. Or if you know the *Look, Say, Cover, Write, Check method* then use that, OK?

➜ All the words in the exercise above are key words and have a small word inside them that you can use as a memory trick to help you spell them. Next, we're going to look at these words within words.

Words within Words

Key words: address, accident, appears/disappears, believe, business, calendar, difficult, different, favourite, heard, heart, island, learn, medicine, peculiar, position, pressure, opposite, separate

→ Let's start getting to know and make friends with some key words that you need to learn.

→ The strategies/memory tricks we're looking at in this section are very good for remembering spellings. You might like some of these and want to use them, or you might not like some of them — that's fine. Use whatever helps you remember a spelling.

→ Seeing words within words can help you remember the difficult bits of the word — the tricky letter patterns (-ie- or -ei-), the silent letters, double consonants, and how to choose which homophone is which.

Exercise

Can you see the **small word within** these tricky words?

For example, *believe* — when you don't tell the truth: <u>lie</u>

1. *separate* — an animal (a rodent) is in this word: _____

2. *business* — you can travel to work on this: _____

3. *peculiar* — someone who doesn't tell the truth is a _____

4. *position* — the opposite of stand is to _____

Top tip: → If you don't understand a word, use a dictionary.

13

→ Seeing a small word within tricky words can help you spell them, especially if the small word is somehow related to the big word (check the words below to see what I mean).

Answers

1. believe — when you don't tell the truth: <u>lie</u>

2. separate — an animal is in this word: <u>rat</u>

3. business — you can travel to work on this: <u>bus</u>

4. peculiar — someone who doesn't tell the truth is a <u>liar</u>

5. position — the opposite of stand is to <u>sit</u>

We're going to connect these small words within words to a sentence to help us remember a spelling and its memory trick. You can draw pictures to help too.

→ See the small word with the -ie- pattern in believe  and connect it to a sentence: *Never be**lie**ve a lie.*
Write your memory tricks and do some *word art* **for believe.**

Remember to spot the vowels believe.
Do you believe **I** exist?
Believe Eve the alien.

→ Can you think of your own **memory tricks** for these words within words? It doesn't matter how crazy your 'tricks' are as long as they help you remember the tricky spelling.

Write your memory tricks and do some *word art.*

→ **separate**
See the rat in <u>**separate**</u>
Separate a rat.

Spot the vowels too:
separate

→ **business**

It's good <u>bus**iness**</u> to go by bus.

Careful, **busyness** means being very busy, very active — *School started and the busyness began.*

→ **peculiar**

He's a <u>pecu**liar**</u> liar.

Liar, liar, pants on fire — what a pecu**liar** sentence!   He's a *familiar peculiar* liar.

→**position** — Sit in this <u>position</u>.

→**opposite** — I sit **opposite** her.

→ **pressure**   See the two words within **pressure**: **press** and sure.

The pressure can **press** on you.

The pressure can **sure** press on you.

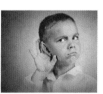Remembering the **press** in pressure helps with the double 's'.

→ **heard**

  ear — hear — <u>heard</u>

Hear with your **ear** and learn.

→ **appears/disappears**

There <u>appears</u> to be an **app** in my **ear**.

→ disappear

→ address

I need to add an add**ress**.

→ heart

My <u>heart</u> is in art.

→ favourite

Our **<u>favourite</u>** flavour.

→ calendar

Len checks his <u>calendar</u> every day.
A **<u>calendar</u>** is a list of dates.

→ accident

When two cars collide, they make a dent.
A car crash makes an instant dent.

→ island

An <u>island</u> is land surrounded by water.

→ **bicycle**

When it's icy, don't ride your <u>bicycle</u>.

→ **different** and **difficult**   (Spot the vowels too.)

→ **diffe**rent — rent

Let's rent a **diff**erent film.

Every Friday film night, we rent a different film.

→ Friday's film about a zombie killer **cult** is **difficult** to watch.

→ **purpose** and **suppose**

There's a **pose** in suppose and pur**pose**.
What do you **suppose** is the **purpose** of his **pose**?

→ **medicine**

There's a **medic** in medicine.

hard c ("k" sound) — medic, medical, medicate, paramedic

soft c ("s" sound) — medicine

→ **argument**

argue but <u>argument</u>

Don't chew **gum** in an **argument**.

Argue → drop the 'e' when *arguing* and having an ***argument***.

Exercise. Write the missing words in the gaps:

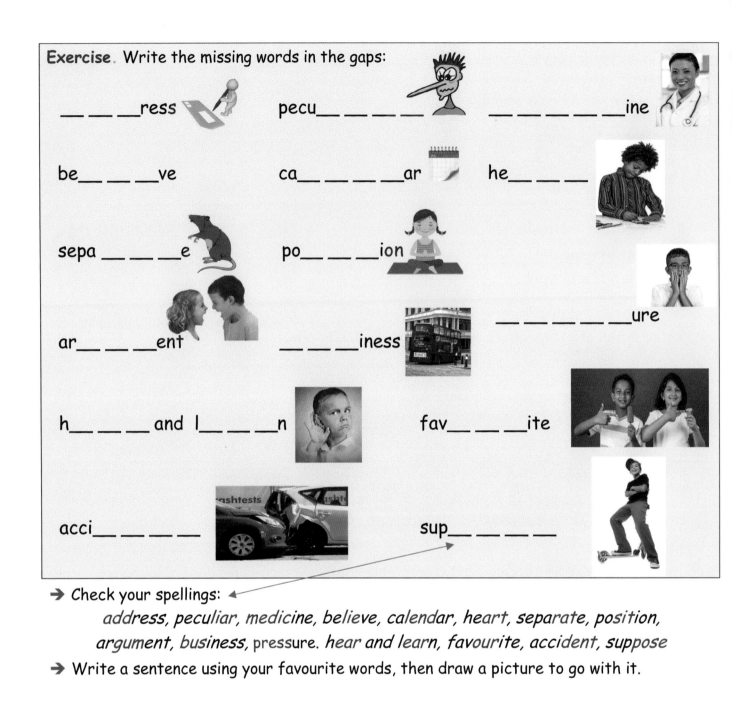

_ _ _ _ress

pecu_ _ _ _

_ _ _ _ _ _ _ine

be_ _ _ _ve

ca_ _ _ _ar

he_ _ _ _

sepa _ _ _ _e

po_ _ _ _ion

ar_ _ _ _ent

_ _ _ _iness

_ _ _ _ _ _ _ure

h_ _ _ _ and l_ _ _ _n

fav_ _ _ _ite

acci_ _ _ _ _

sup_ _ _ _ _

→ Check your spellings:

*address, peculiar, medicine, believe, calendar, heart, separate, position,
argument, business,* pressure. *hear and learn, favourite, accident, suppose*

→ Write a sentence using your favourite words, then draw a picture to go with it.

_____

_____

18

Write the missing words in the gap:

For example: **Add** an address.   The **pressure** can _____ on you.

A _____ will give you **medicine**.   That's _____ favourite.

Don't have an **argument** while chewing _____.   Separate a _____.

He's a peculiar _____.   Don't believe a _____.

I h**ear** with my _____ and l**earn**.   _____ in a comfortable position.

It's good **business** to go by _____.   Can you _____ me a ca**lendar**?

Let's _____ a diff**erent** movie.   The car has a _____ since the acci**dent**.

Word Search

Words can go forwards, backwards, diagonally, vertically or horizontally!

This one is tricky — can you do it? I bet you can, but it's going to make you go ➡

address
appears
~~believe~~
business
calendar
different
difficult
disappears
favourite
heard
heart
island
learn
opposite
peculiar
position
separate

```
m g k t s r i x y e r m n p s
u h r e m x u e l h a a o m z
d i s a p p e a r s d r i u o
b f d o d w t s i s n a t p a
s u k v g n e e s q e i i o w
d e s l t p a e b d l l s o w
i i v i a n r l s y a u o f q
h p f r n d e r s r c c p a y
i e a f d e a r i i d e l v v
y t a a i e s b e s d p e o h
e i g r p c a s r f m m a u e
m a n p t t u f s c f c r r a
y h a i r m d l q r g i n i r
e t i s o p p o t v u u d t d
b e l i e v e d p r a l d e r
```

19

Exercise

Use the word-within-word trick or spotting the vowels method to decide which is correct.

1. a. medicine
   b. medisine

2. a. peculier
   b. peculiar

3. a. grammer
   b. grammar

4. a. remember
   b. remembar

5. a. experiance
   b. experience

6. a. accident
   b. accidant

7. a. argument
   b. arguement

8. a. calendar
   b. calandar

9. a. beleive
   b. believe

10. a. business
    b. buisiness

11. a. favarite
    b. favourite

12. a. apears
    b. appears

13. a. seperate
    b. separate

14. a. adress
    b. address

15. a. different
    b. differant

16. a. presure
    b. pressure

Exercise

Find the word within the word. Underline it. Write it out.

For example: Underline an *animal* in **edu<u>cat</u>ion**: <u>cat</u>

1. Underline something that's *not true* in **believe**: _____

2. Underline a *past tense verb* meaning *end of life* in **studied**: _____

3. Underline a type of *transport* in **business**: _____

4. Underline the *final part* in **friend**: _____

5. Underline *a part of the head* in **learn**: _____

6. Underline a *number* in **money**: _____

7. Underline another word for *everything* in **usually**: _____

8. Underline another word for *hello* in **while**: _____

Answers

1. a. medicine
   b. ~~medisine~~

2. ~~a. peculier~~
   b. peculiar

3. ~~a. grammer~~
   b. grammar

4. a. remember
   b. ~~remembar~~

5. ~~a. experiance~~
   b. experience

6. a. accident
   b. ~~accidant~~

7. a. argument
   b. ~~arguement~~

8. a. calendar
   b. ~~calandar~~

9. ~~a. beleive~~
   b. believe

10. a. business
    b. ~~buisiness~~

11. ~~a. favarite~~
    b. favourite

12. ~~a. apears~~
    b. appears

13. ~~a. seperate~~
    b. separate

14. ~~a. adress~~
    b. address

15. a. different
    b. ~~differant~~

16. ~~a. presure~~
    b. pressure

→ Write a sentence with some of these words.

_____

_____

Answers

1. Underline something that's *not true* in **believe**: <u>lie</u>

2. Underline a *past tense verb* meaning *end of life* in **studied**: <u>died</u>

3. Underline a type of *transport* in **business**: <u>bus</u>

4. Underline the *final part* in **friend**: <u>end</u>

5. Underline *a part of the head* in **learn**: <u>ear</u>

6. Underline a *number* in **money**: <u>one</u>

7. Underline another word for *everything* in **usually**: <u>all</u>

8. Underline another word for *hello* in **while**: <u>hi</u>

Adapted from Johanna Stirling's *Teaching Spelling to English Learners* book

Key word revision. Fill in the missing letters: Carefully check you've filled them in correctly.

1. __ __ __ress, __ddr__ss, a__ __ __e__ __, ad__ __ __ __ __ __, __ __ __ __ __ __

2. be__ __ __ve, b__l__ __v__, __e__ie__e, beli__ __ __, __ __ __ __ __ __ __

3. ca__ __ __ __ar, c__l__nd__r, __a__e__ __a__, __ __ __ __ __ __ __

4. diffi__ __ __ __, d__ff__c__lt, __i__ __i__u__ __, __ __ __ __ __ __ __ __

5. diffe__ __ __ __, d__ff__r__nt, __i__ __e__e__ __, __ __ __ __ __ __ __ __

6. fav__ __ __ite, f__v__ __r__t__, __a__ou__i__e, __ __ __ __ __ __ __ __ __

7. h__ __ __d, __ea__ __, hea__ __, __ __ __ __ __ __ __ __ __ __

8. h__ __ __t, __ea__ __, hea__ __, __ __ __ __ __ __ __ __

9. l__ __ __n, __ea__ __, lea__ __, __ __ __ __ __ __ __ __

10. __ __land, is__ __ __ __ __, __sl__nd, i__ __a__ __, __ __ __ __ __ __ __ __ __

11. pecu__ __ __ __, p__c__l__ __r, __e__u__ia__, __ __ __ __ __ __ __ __ __ __

12. sepa__ __ __e, sep__r__te, s__parat__, __e__a__a__e, __ __ __ __ __ __ __ __

Homophone Preparation

In the next section, we're going to look at **homophones**.

→ Do you know what **homophones** are? Check these homophones out. What do you notice when you read them out loud?

> **peace/piece, plain/plane, weight/wait, caught/court, through/threw,**
>
> **grown/groan, break/brake, herd/heard, rain/reign**

→ Did you notice how they have the same sound but different spellings and meanings?

We're going to look at how using words within words and other memory tricks can help us figure out which homophone to use.

→ **Homophone preparation exercise**

→ Read these and decide which word in bold is correct. Cross out the incorrect ones.

→ If you don't know or are not sure, then don't worry. We're going to look at how to figure out which word to use later.

1. I'd like a **piece/peace** of that cake but if I get **court/caught**, they'll **groan/grown** at me.

2. It's **plane/plain** to see he really wants a **peace/piece** of that cake.

3. She's listening to music **threw/through** her headphones.

4. The **plane/plain** is landing.

5. I want a **break/brake** from all this homework.

Remembering Which Homophone is Which

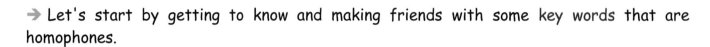

Which witch is which?

Key words: weight, reign, caught, heard, through

➔ Let's start by getting to know and making friends with some key words that are homophones.

➔ Read these out loud and notice how they have the same sound but different spellings and meanings:

weight/wait	which/witch	weather/whether	caught/court
reign/rein	whose/who's	meat/meet	threw/through
male/mail	to/too/two	heard/herd	heal/heel/he'll
mane/main	groan/grown	break/brake	

➔ These are **homophones**.

Homophones are words with the same sound but different meanings and different spellings.

There are hundreds of homophones in English and knowing which homophone to use can be difficult.

Sometimes when we write quickly, we write the first homophone that comes into our brain. That's why it's so important to re-read your work to check you've used the right one.

Answers

1. I'd like a **piece** of that cake but if I get **caught**, they'll **groan** at me.

2. It's **plain** to see he really wants a **piece** of that cake.

3. She's listening to music **through** her headphones.

4. The **plane** is landing.

5. I want a **break** from all this homework.

➔ Please note that if you don't have any problems knowing which word is which, then move on and work on the words that are a problem.

→ Seeing words **within** words and **using a relevant saying** is excellent for remembering which **homophone** is which. **Spotting vowels** and noticing letter patterns are great too.

Write your memory tricks **and do some** *word art.*

peace / piece
→ peace is ace
→ piece of pie

plain / plane
→ A plain white T-shirt.
→ Land a plane in a lane.

grown / groan
→ I'm all **grown** up and can stay home on my **own**.
→ To **moan** and **groan** is so annoying.

brake / break
→ He had to brake hard to avoid slamming into the idiot and his car's brakes screeched.
→ You **break** your nightly **fast** at breakfast, so **eat** a good breakfast.
tea break, coffee break, weekend break, lunch break

hear / here

➜ Hear with your **ear** and learn.

➜ **Here**, there, where, everywhere.

meet / meat

➜ **Meet** me at the next **meet**ing.

➜ Take a seat and let's **eat meat**.

Exercise

Fill in the gaps with the correct homophone.

1. (peace/piece)

She's at _____ with herself while she's in her _____ of heaven — on her boat.

2. (hear/here) Can you _____ that noise coming from right _____?

3. (meat/meet) Do you eat _____? If so, let's _____ at the Beefeater.

4. (brake/break)

   He slammed his foot on the _____ so he didn't _____ the speed limit.

5. (groan/grown) When I'm a _____-up, I won't moan and _____.

6. (plane/plain) When I'm on a _____, I like to eat _____ food.

Answers

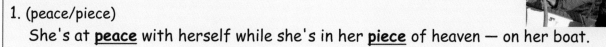

1. (peace/piece)

   She's at **peace** with herself while she's in her **piece** of heaven — on her boat.

2. (hear/here) Can you **hear** that noise coming from right **here**?

3. (meat/meet) Do you eat **meat**? If so, let's **meet** at the Beefeater.

4. (brake/break) He slammed his foot on the **brake** so he didn't **break** the speed limit.

5. (groan/grown) When I'm a **grown**-up, I won't moan and **groan**.

6. (plane/plain) When I'm on a **plane**, I like to eat **plain** food.

➔ Write a couple of sentences like these and draw a picture too.

_____

_____

_____

Key words: weight, reign, caught, heard, through

The key homophones you need to learn have some difficult vowel patterns in them:

weight, reign, caught, heard, through

These are some of the trickiest words to spell. But they're easy to learn with some memory tricks. Before we dive into the tips, do you know what these words mean?

Word study: weight, reign, caught, heard, through

1. Which is the past tense of *catch?* _____

2. Which is the past tense of *hear?* _____

3. Which is about kings and queens ruling a country? _____

4. Which is a measurement of how heavy something or someone is? _____

5. Which means going from one end to the other? _____

➜ Draw a line to the picture that has something to do with the words:

weight, reign, caught, heard, through

➔Do some *word art* for *weight, reign, caught, heard, through:*

➔Write a sentence for these words.

<u>I **caught** the ball and we won the match.</u>

_____

(weight) _____

_____ (heard)

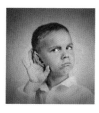

(reign)_____

_____(through)

➔Do you know the homophone partners that go with these words — caught, weight, heard, reign, through?

➔Read them out loud to help. Have a guess. It's fine if you're wrong or don't know.

➔Here are some picture clues:

1. **weight** and wait

2. **reign** (two other words!) and

    or

3. **caught** and

4. **heard** and

5. **through** and

Answers

➔ 1. weight/**wait**   *To **wait** for a bus is so boring.*

➔ 2. reign/**rein/rain**   *It always seems to **rain** at weekends.   Pull the left **rein** to turn left.*

➔ 3. caught/**court**   *This is Centre **Court** at Wimbledon.*

➔ 4. heard/**herd**   *A lovely **herd** of cows.*

➔ 5. through/**threw**   *They **threw** their planes in the air.*

Exercise
wait, rein, rain, threw, court, herd

1. Which one is the past tense of **throw**? _____

2. Which one means a large group of animals (or zombies)? _____

3. Which one means a place for sport or criminal trials? _____

4. Which one means a thin piece of leather that helps to steer a horse? _____

5. Which one means wet weather? _____

6. Which one means stay in one place or delay doing something? _____

➔**Let's study these words and look at some memory tricks.**

Word study: weight/wait

Write your memory tricks and do some *word art.*

*If you can't **wait** to lose **weight**, start **weight**lifting.*

weight
My **weight** isn't eight stone.
Weights for **weight**lifting.

wait
Wait for the fish to take the bait.

Fill in the missing letters:

➔ w__ __ght,   wei__ __t,   __ei__ __ __,   _____

➔ w__ __t,   w__ __ __,   __ai__,   _____

➔Write a sentence with both words if you can.

_____

_____

Write your memory tricks and do some *word art.*

reign — The glorious reign of Elizabeth II.
Queen Elizabeth **reigns** *over the UK.*
The silent 'g' shows that it comes from Latin (*regnum*)
for 'king, kingship, rule'.
In America, baseball **reigns** *supreme.*
She's the **reigning** *Olympic champion.*

rein — Hold onto the reins tightly.
reins are usually a long, thin piece of leather to control and direct a horse.
You pull on both **reins** *to stop or slow a horse, but only the left* **rein**
to turn left.

rain — It's a p**ai**n when it r**ai**ns, especially when you're on holiday in Sp**ai**n.

Fill in the missing letters:

➔ r__ __gn,   __ei__ __,   r__ __ __ __,   _____

➔ re __n,   __ei__,   r__ __ __,   _____

➔ ra __n,   __ai__,   r__ __ __,   _____

➔ Write a sentence with these words.

_____

_____

Word study: caught/court

Don't get **caught** *or you'll end up in* **court.** **Write your** memory tricks **and do some** *word art.*

---

caught

Caught is the past tense of *catch.*
I caught the ball and we won the game.
caught sounds and looks like: taught, daughter, slaughter

---

court

A **court** of law.
The **court** of Henry the VIII.
tennis **court**, basketball court, badminton court,
courtyard

Fill in the missing letters:

➔ c__ __ght, cau__ __ __, __au__ __ __, c__ __ __ __t, _____

➔ c__ __rt, cou__ __, __ou__ __, c__ __ __t, _____

➔ Write a sentence with both words in it if you can.

_____

_____

Word study: heard/herd

*I **heard** about a lovely **herd** of cows.*   **Write your** memory **tricks and do some** *word art.*

heard

Heard is the past tense of **hear**.

I **heard** a strange sound last night.

Hear with your ear. I heard that!

herd

a **herd** of elephants, a **herd** of cows, a **herd** of zombies

I'm a nerd and like the herd of zombies on *Walking Dead.*

Fill in the missing letters:

→ h__ __ __d, __ea__ __, __ __ __ __d, _____

→ h__ __d, h__rd, he__ __, h __ __ __, _____

→Write a sentence with both words in it if you can.

_____

_____

Word study: through/threw

*He **threw** the ball right **through** the hoop.*

Your memory tricks **and** *word art.*

through

*I enjoy walking **through** the park with my parents.*

➜ Notice the '**thr**' pattern (**through**, **three**, **throw**, **threw**, **throat**).
➜ We can use a *verb + through: click through, walk through, go through, run through, cut through, squeeze through, look through, think through...*

Go around or through the rough grass in the park.

threw

Threw is the past tense of throw.

throw — threw

Threw sounds and looks like: brew, screw, drew, crew, chew, few, new, knew, flew, etc.

Fill in the missing letters:

➜ thr__w, thr__ __, __ __ __ew, _____

➜ thr__ __gh, th__ __ __ __ __ __, __ __ __ough, __ __rou__ __, _____

➜ Write a sentence with both words in it if you can.

_____

_____

→**Proofreading** is a very important skill to develop.

Proofreading your writing means going over your work slowly to spot errors, to see if the sentences sound right, to check if there are no missing words and letters, and to see if you've used the right homophones.

Exercise

Are the homophones in bold correct or incorrect? Rewrite the homophone errors*. Use your memory tricks to help.

1. We went **threw** the park on our way home.

2. I hope you didn't **wait** too long.

3. I went fishing and **caught** a big trout.

4. I'm fed up with all this **rein** and want to play outside.

5. I **herd** the news this morning and it was depressing.

6. I **court** the ball and we won the match.

7. I go **through** the park on my way to school.

8. During his **reign** as manager, England won the European and World Cups.

Clue: There are four sentences that have the correct homophone.

*You're only just learning these words so don't be hard on yourself if you can't decide which is right or not.

Learning anything takes a few goes and a bit of brainpower so go over the previous pages again.

Answers

      through
1. We went ~~threw~~ the park on our way home.

2. I hope you didn't **wait** too long. ✓

3. I went fishing and **caught** a big trout. ✓

      rain
4. I'm fed up with all this ~~rein~~ and want to play outside.

  heard
5. I ~~herd~~ the news this morning and it was depressing.

  caught
6. I ~~court~~ the ball and we won the match.

7. I go **through** the park on my way to school. ✓

8. During his **reign** as manager, England won the European and World Cups. ✓

Do you need to revise any of these words?

➔ **Prefixes, root words and suffixes preparation**

In the next section, we'll be looking at **prefixes**, **root words**, and **suffixes**. Knowing these and noticing them will help you spell and read long words.

Do you know what **prefixes**, **root words**, and **suffixes** are?

Look at these words and see how they are built with a **prefix**, **root word** and **suffix**. Add these words to the diagram below.

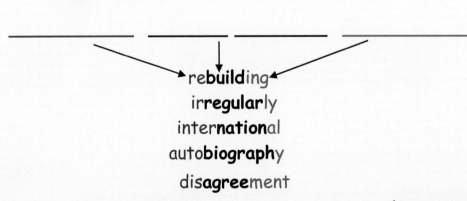

(Answers on the next page.)

Building Words with Root Words, Prefixes and Suffixes

Never be scared of long words ever again — read on.

→ Let's start getting to know and making friends with prefixes and suffixes. These are fantastic friends to have because they can help us spell and read long words instead of getting scared of them.

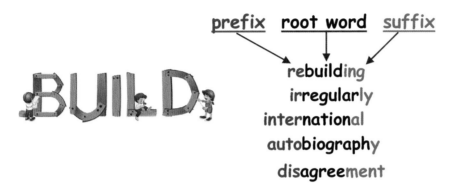

prefix   root word   suffix

rebuilding
irregularly
international
autobiography
disagreement

We add **prefixes** and **suffixes** to **root words** (complete words).

Prefixes are little words we add to the beginning of root words to make the word negative or to add extra information.

We're going to look at some prefixes that are important to learn: **un, dis, re, in, mis, super, anti, auto, im, il.**

disagree, unhealthy, unlucky, superman/Superman, superpower
immature, impossible, insane, incorrect
autopilot, anticlockwise, illegal

We add prefixes to the beginning of root words, usually without any changes in spelling. There are hundreds of prefixes. Some of the most popular are: **in-, un-, dis-, mis-, ir-, il-, im-, pre-, ex-, anti-, uni-**

→ Some common prefixes are **un-, re-, in-, dis-, mis-**   Write a couple of words with these.

Prefixes

un-, re-, in-, dis-, mis- prefixes

→ **un-** (not) → **un** + happy = **unhappy** = **not** happy
unusual, uncomfortable, unbelievable, unnatural, unsure, uncertain, unfriendly, unknown, uneasy, unhealthy, unsteady, unfair, unlucky, unpopular

→ **re-** (do something again, repeat, return, go back)
→ **re** + paint = **repaint** = paint (it/these) again
redo, retry, rebuild, replay, reappear, redecorate, refresh, reuse, recycle, rewrite, react, return

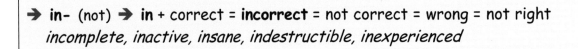

→ **in-** (not) → **in** + correct = **incorrect** = not correct = wrong = not right
incomplete, inactive, insane, indestructible, inexperienced

→ **dis-** (to make opposite, negative) → **dis** + appear = **disappear** = not be seen
disagree, disobey, disappoint, dishonest, dissatisfied, discontinued

→ **mis-** (done wrong/badly) → **mis** + behave = **misbehave** = behave badly
mislead, misspell, mismanage, misguide, misdirect, misplace

Exercise

→Write the meanings of these words: For example, *unsure* = <u>not sure</u>, *redo* = <u>do it again</u>

1. unhealthy = _____

2. rewrite = _____

3. incomplete = _____

4. unpopular = _____

5. ungrateful = _____

6. redo = _____

7. unfair = _____

8. uncomfortable = _____

9. reuse = _____

10. inactive = _____

Answers

1. unhealthy = <u>not healthy</u>
2. rewrite = <u>write it again</u>
3. incomplete = <u>not complete</u>
4. unpopular = <u>not popular</u>
5. ungrateful = <u>not grateful</u>
6. redo = <u>do it again</u>
7. unfair = <u>not fair</u>
8. uncomfortable = <u>not comfortable</u>
9. reuse = <u>use it again</u>
10. inactive = <u>not active</u>

➔ Notice the double letters in the following words. We add a prefix to the root word which creates double letters:◄

dis + satisfied = di<u>ss</u>atisfied

mis + spell = mi<u>ss</u>pell

im + mature = i<u>mm</u>ature

il + legal = i<u>ll</u>egal

ir + responsible = i<u>rr</u>esponsible

ir + regular = i<u>rr</u>egular

un + natural = u<u>nn</u>atural

➔ **Remember to use a dictionary if you don't understand a word.**

Some prefixes have opposites:

in / ex	in / de	im / ex
include / **ex**clude	**in**flate / **de**flate	**im**port / **ex**port
inhale / **ex**hale	**in**crease / **de**crease	**im**plode / **ex**plode

Prefix rules

➔ Can you see the prefix rules in these words?

➔ illegal, illegible

➔ irregular, irresponsible

➔ immature, immortal

➔ impossible, impatient

*He's an **immortal** and so **impatient,** but thank goodness he's not **immature** or **irresponsible**.*

Prefix Rules and Exceptions

There are plenty of exceptions to these rules, but pronunciation can help.

Use **il** before words starting with **l**:

legal — **il**legal   *That's not legal — that's illegal.*

legible — **il**legible   *I can't read this — it's illegible.*

logical — **il**logical   *That's stupid and doesn't make sense — it's totally illogical.*

(But *unlawful, unless* — the 'un' helps the pronunciation.)

Use **ir** before words starting with **r**:

relevant — **ir**relevant   *That question is not important — it's totally irrelevant.*

regular — **ir**regular   *She works different shifts and her hours are irregular.*

responsible — **ir**responsible   *His behaviour was so irresponsible.*

(But *unreal, unrated* — the 'un' helps the pronunciation.)

Use **im** before words starting with **m** and **p**:

mature — **im**mature   *My dad's so immature — I'm the mature one!*

mortal — **im**mortal   *Vampires are immortal and live forever until staked!*

material — **im**material   *The age difference is immaterial* (not important).

possible — **im**possible   *Everything is possible even though you think it's impossible.*

perfect — **im**perfect   *We're living in an imperfect world.*

patient — **im**patient   *He gets impatient with people who don't agree with him.*

(But *unmarked, unmarried, unpack, unpick, unpaid*
— the 'un' helps the pronunciation.)

➔ **Remember to use a dictionary if you don't understand a word.**

Exercise 1. Add a prefix to these words. For example, **not regular** = _irregular_

not possible = _____

not perfect = _____

not patient = _____

not mature = _____

not relevant = _____

not legal = _____

not logical = _____

not regular = _____

Check your spellings against the list of words on the previous page.

Exercise 2. Add **un**, **re**, **im**, **in** or **dis** to these key words: (Answers on the next page.)

1. _____popular   2. _____appear   3. _____natural   4. _____continue

5. _____certain   6. _____possible   7. _____complete   8. _____important

➔ Choose your favourite word and do some _word art._

➔ Write a sentence with some of these words.

_____

_____

What do you think these prefixes mean? Have a guess.

sub- (submarine, submerge)   **super**- (superhero, superstar)

anti- (antisocial, antivirus)   **auto**- (autograph, autobiography)

inter- (intergalactic, intercity)

  It's perfectly OK if you don't know. We're going to look at these next.

Common prefixes

sub- means 'under' or 'close to'
submarine, submerge, subway, subdivide, subheading

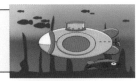

super- means 'above', beyond', 'very big'
supermarket, superstore, superstar, supermodel, supersonic, superpower, superhero, superhuman, supercool

anti- means 'against'
antiseptic, anticlockwise, antisocial, antivirus

auto- means 'by yourself/itself'
autobiography, autograph, autopilot, automatic

inter- means 'between' or 'among'
interaction, intercity, international, interface, interactive, intergalactic (between two galaxies),   *interactive whiteboard*

Rewrite and add the correct prefix (sub, super, anti, auto, inter).

national — <u>international</u>

1. sonic — _____

2. biography — _____

3. merge — _____

4. hero — _____

5. active — _____

6. virus — _____

Answers

1. sonic — <u>supersonic</u>
2. biography — <u>autobiography</u>
3. merge — <u>submerge</u>
4. hero — <u>superhero</u>
5. active — <u>interactive</u>
6. virus — <u>antivirus</u>

Suffixes

Don't forget your **suffixes** and **spelling rules**. A suffix is added to the end of a word to turn it into another word. Suffixes make words even longer.

➔ Sometimes we can add a **suffix** to a **root word** without changing anything:

usual — usually — unusually

fresh — refreshed — refreshing — refreshes

build — builder — building — rebuilds — rebuilding

nation — nations — national — nationality — international

appear — appears — appearing — disappears — disappearance

act — acts — acting — acted — active — action — reacts — reacting — reacted — reaction

➔ **Drop the 'e' rule** with **vowel suffixes** (more details in the next chapter):

behave — behaving — misbehaving

nature — natural — unnatural

believe — believable — unbelievable

adventure — adventurous — unadventurous

arrange — arranging — arranged — rearranged

continue — continued — continuing — continual

> ➔ Do you know which is correct and **why**? Have a guess (see page 47).
> a. writing   b. writeing
> a. excitment   b. excitement
> a. famous   b. fameous
> a. lovely   b. lovly

➔ **Doubling up rule with** vowels suffixes (more details about this rule later):

forget — forgetting — unforgettable

quiz — quizzes — quizzing — quizzed

stop — stopped — stopping — stopper — stoppable — stoppage — unstoppable

➔ **'y' to 'i' rule** if the root word has more than one syllable:

beauty — beautiful, penny — penniless

happy — happily — unhappily — happiness — unhappiness

Exercise

Rewrite and use different colours to separate the **prefix**, **root word** and **suffix**.

*rebuilding ➜ <u>rebuilding</u> = re + build + ing

Remember, we drop the 'e' in some root words:

*unbelievable ➜ <u>unbelievable</u> = un + believe + able

	Write the root word here.
	<u>build</u>
	<u>believe</u>

*discontinued _____ _____

*disappearance _____ _____

*unnoticed _____ _____

*irregularly _____ _____

*incompletely _____ _____

*inexperienced _____ _____

 disagreement _____ _____

anticlockwise _____ _____

international _____ _____

unfriendly _____ _____

*undecided _____ _____

The words with an asterisk (*) have **root words** that are key words.

Answers	root words *key words
rebuilding — re**build**ing = re + **build** + ing ⟶	build*
unbelievable — un**believ**able = un + **believe** + able	believe*
discontinued — dis**continu**ed = dis + **continue** + ed	continue*
disappearance — dis**appear**ance = dis + **appear** + ance	appear*
unnoticed — un**notic**ed = un + **notice** + ed	notice*
irregularly — ir**regular**ly = ir + **regular** + ly	regular*
incompletely — in**complete**ly = in + **complete** + ly	complete*
inexperienced — in**experienc**ed = in + **experience** + ed	experience*
disagreement — dis**agree**ment = dis + **agree** + ment	agree
anticlockwise — anti**clock**wise = anti + **clock** + wise	clock
international — inter**nation**al = inter + **nation** + al	nation
unfriendly — un**friend**ly = un + **friend** + ly	friend
undecided — un**decid**ed = un + **decide**+ ed	decide*

Spelling Rules

Drop the 'e'

Answers

a. writing   b. excitement   a. famous   b. lovely

➜ Notice the vowel and consonant suffixes:

<u>drop the **e**</u>	<u>keep the **e**</u>
write ➜ writing	love ➜ lovely
fame ➜ famous	excite ➜ excitement

➜ Drop the 'e' when adding a **vowel suffix** ending: **-ing**, **-ous**, **-ed**, **-er**, **-est**, **-ize**, **-or**

write + **ing** = *writing*   arrive — *arrival, arriving, arrived*

fame + **ous** = *famous*   believe — *believing, believer, believable, unbelievable*

➜**Y** is sometimes a vowel. When we add 'y' to the end of words, it becomes a vowel suffix and we drop the **e**: ease + y = easy, laze + y = lazy, shake — shaky, stone — stony, slime — slimy

---

➜**Keep the 'e'** when adding a consonant suffix ending: **-ly**, **-ment**, **-s**, **-ful**, **-less**, **-ness**... (with some exceptions we'll see on the next page).

excite + **ment** = *excitement* (keep the "e")   love + **ly** = lovely (keep the "e")

lively, writes, hopeful, hopeless, tasteless, blueness

The drop the 'e' rule is a great little rule to know, but be warned: like all English spelling rules, there are exceptions.

Common exceptions

➔For words ending in -**ue**, we drop the "e" with –ly:

true — truly,   due — duly

truly is often misspelt: true + ly = *truly* (drop the "e")

It's truly hot in July.

➔We drop the "e" in *argument* — argue + ment = **argument**

See the "gum" in ar**gum**ent — *Don't chew **gum** in an ar**gum**ent.*

➔**Drop the 'e' spelling rule**

When we add a **vowel suffix** (-ing, -er, -al, -ed, -ant, -es, -ent, -ation, -ous) to words ending in 'e', we usually drop the 'e'.

➔Rewrite these key words and add some vowel suffixes (-ing, -al, -ed, -ation, -ion).

For example: arrive — <u>arriving, arrival</u>

believe — _____

centre — _____

circle — _____

complete — _____

guide — _____

decide — _____

describe — _____

imagine — _____

argue — _____

Answers on the next page.

Some possible answers

arrive — arriving, arrival, arrived

believe — believing, believed

centre — central, centred

circle — circling, circled

complete — completing, completed, completion

guide — guiding, guided

decide — deciding, decided, undecided

describe — describing, described

imagine — imagining, imagined, imagination

exercise — exercising, exercised

argue — arguing, argued, (argument)

More key words

breathe — breathing, breathed

continue — continuing, continued, continual

fame — famed, famous

increase — increased, increasing

nature — natural, unnatural

opposite — opposition

pressure — pressuring, pressured

promise — promising, promised

separate — separating, separated

suppose — supposing, supposed

surprise — surprising, surprised

experience — experienced, experiencing, inexperienced

➔ Adding -ly preparation

Next, we're going to look at adding the suffix **-ly** to words and how we keep and change the 'e', and also drop the 'e' on one important word.

Key words
Which is correct?

1. a. probably	2. a. actualy	3. a. lovely	4. a. accidentaly	5. a. happyly
b. probablely	b. actually	b. lovly	b. accidentally	b. happily

49

Adding -ly to Words

Key words: **accidentally, actually, occasionally, probably**

> I **occasionally** read a book, but I **probably** should read more because
> I **actually** enjoy reading.

'ly' is added to an **adjective** to make **adverbs**: certain + ly = **certainly**, useful + ly = **usefully**.

Rule 1: *I hope this is going **smoothly** so far.*

    Add **ly** to most words (-ly):

slow + ly = slowly

recent — recently

stupid — stupidly

certain — certainly

sad — sadly

quick — quickly

quiet — quietly

loud — loudly

important — importantly

kind / unkind — kindly / unkindly

friend — friendly, unfriendly

*If you need to go **slowly**, that's fine.*

Rule 2: *Actually, this **really** is a **totally** easy rule.*

    Add **ly** to words ending in 'l' (-lly) (this makes double 'l'):

cool + ly = coolly

real + ly = really

wool — woolly

faithful — faithfully

Notice these -ally patterns:

usual + ly = usually

real + ly = really

final + ly = finally

total — totally

Key words: actual — actually, accidental — accidentally, occasional — occasionally

Rule 3: *Carefully does it and **hopefully** you'll understand.*

Adding **ly** to words ending in -**ful** makes -**fully** (notice the double 'l'):

careful + ly = carefully

beautiful + ly = beautifully

successful — successfully

playful — playfully

hopeful — hopefully

thoughtful — thoughtfully

*That was **beautifully** done! Now that you've **successfully** read this, go to the next page.*

Rule 4: It's ***lovely*** to feel ***completely*** happy.

Keep the 'e' (-**ely**):

lone + ly = lonely

love + ly = lovely

live + ly = lively

like + ly = likely

close — closely

nice — nicely

safe — safely

sure — surely

strange — strangely

complete — completely

extreme — extremely

separate — separately

Exceptions: Drop the 'e' in:

true + ly = ***truly*** ⟸ **Truly** is one of the most misspelt words in English.

due + ly = duly   *(It's truly hot in July.)*

whole + ly = wholly

Rule 5: *This **probably** looks **incredibly** hard.*

Change the **e** to **y** in words ending in a consonant + **le** (-**ly**): probable — probably

gentle — gently   possible — possibly   terrible — terribly

simple — simply   responsible — responsibly   horrible — horribly

incredible — incredibly   humble — humbly   sensible — sensibly

Rule 6: *Luckily, this is nearly the end.*

crazy — crazily

For two-syllable words ending in a consonant + y, change the y to i (**-ily**):

easy — easily, uneasily
angry — angrily
happy — happily, unhappily
busy — busily
crazy — crazily
lazy — lazily
ready — readily
hungry — hungrily
ordinary — ordinarily
noisy — noisily
lucky — luckily, unluckily

But keep the 'y' in one syllable words:

shy + ly = shyly
sly + ly = slyly
dry + ly = dryly or drily

Rule 7: Add **–ally** to words ending in **-ic** (**-ically**):

bas**ic** + ally = *basically*   com**ic** + ally = *comically*   dramatic — *dramatically*

magically, medically, musically, frantically

A big exception is *publicly = public + ly*

If a word ends in **-al**, just add **ly** (**-ally**):

accidental ➔ accidentally   occasional ➔ occasionally   original ➔ originally
incidental ➔ incidentally   musical ➔ musically   experimental ➔ experimentally

Key words: actual ➔ actually,   accidental ➔ accidentally,   occasional ➔ occasionally

Notice how these key words are built:

act ➔ actual ➔ actu**ally**

accident ➔ accidental ➔ accidentally

occasion ➔ occasional ➔ occasionally

Notice how these words are built:

act → actual → actually

magic → magical → magically

music → musical → musically

drama → dramatic→ dramatical →dramatically

occasion → occasional → occasionally

accident → accidental → accidentally

experiment → experimental → experimentally

continue → (drop the 'e') → continual → continually

nature → (drop the 'e' and add 'al') → natural → naturally

probable → (drop the 'e' and add 'y') → probably

Word study: **actually, accidentally, occasionally, probably**

→ What words within words can you see?

→ Write the vowels in different colours.

→ What memory tricks can you think of?

Word study: Fill in the missing letters:

a__ __identally,   acci__ __ __ __ally,   accident__ __ __ __,

__cc__d__nt__lly,   a__ __i_e__ __a__ __ __,   _____

o__ __asionally,   o__ __a__io__a__ __ __,   occa__ __ __ __ally,

__cc__s__ __n__lly,   _____

__ctu__lly,   a__ __ua__ __ __,   __ct__ __lly,   __ __ __ually,

act__ __ __ __ __,   _____

pr__b__bly,   proba__ __ __,   __ __o__a__ __ __,   pro__ __ __ly,

__ __ __bably,   _____

➔ Do some *word art* for some of these words.

➔ Use one or two of these **key words** in a sentence: **actually, accidentally, occasionally, probably.**

_____

_____

Exercise

Rewrite these and add **ly**. Remember the rules for these.

Remember the rules for these — check on the previous pages if you can't.

For example: certain — <u>certainly</u>

1. love — _____

2. hopeful — _____

3. final — _____

4. complete — _____

5. extreme — _____

6. important — _____

7. particular — _____

8. possible — _____

9. quarter — _____

10. special — _____

11. occasional — _____

12. probable — _____

13. happy — _____

14. basic — _____

15. accident — _____

16. different — _____

17. natural — _____

18. recent — _____

19. regular — _____

20. separate — _____

21. strange — _____

22. crazy — _____

23. actual — _____

24. true — _____

Answers

Check your spelling carefully.

In words ending in 'e', did you keep or change it, or drop it for one key word*?

*Key words.

1. love — **lovely**

2. hopeful — **hopefully**

3. final — **finally**

4. *complete — **completely**

5. * extreme — **extremely**

6. *important — **importantly**

7. *particular — **particularly**

8. *possible — **possibly**

9. *quarter — **quarterly**

10. *special — **specially**

11. *occasional — **occasionally**

12. *probable — **probably**

13. happy — **happily**

14. basic — **basically**

15. *accident — **accidentally**

16. *different — **differently**

17. *natural — **naturally**

18. *recent — **recently**

19. *regular — **regularly**

20. *separate — **separately**

21. *strange — **strangely**

22. crazy — **crazily**

23. *actual — **actually**

24. *true — **truly** (drop the 'e')
    truly is often misspelt

➔ How did you do? Do you need to go over some of these rules or words again?

➔ **Next chapter preparation exercise**
   Which is correct?

1. a. regular   2. a. populer   3. a. particular   4. a. peculiar
   b. reguler   b. popular   b. particuler   b. peculair

-ar Endings

Key words: regular, popular, particular, peculiar ← Answers

-ular endings are adjectives.

*There's a **particular** person in school who is very **popular** and **regularly** gets into trouble.*

Word study: regular, popular, particular

→ Notice the -ular pattern:
*reg**ular**, pop**ular**, partic**ular**, triang**ular**, circ**ular**, molec**ular**...*

→ Breaking these down into syllables can help you spell them.
Say the word slowly and exaggerate the syllables:

"reg-u-lar"

"pop-u-lar"

"par-tic-u-lar"

→ See the small words at the beginning of these: regular, popular, particular
Pop music is the short version of popular music.
This particular part is particularly useful.
Reg is a regular guy.

→ Can you think of any memory tricks, or see any words within the word?

Fill in the missing vowels: r__g__l__r,   p__p__l__r,   p__rt__c__l__r

Spelling rules
Add -ly: regularly, popularly, particularly

→ Do some word art.   → Write a sentence with these words.

Word study: peculiar

-liar endings

Peculiar is a peculiar word.

→ Breaking *peculiar* down into syllables can help you spell it.
   Say the word slowly and exaggerate the syllables: "pe-cu-li-ar"

→ See the small words within words: pecu**liar**. *Liar, liar, pants on fire* — what a peculiar saying! He's a *familiar, peculiar* liar.

→ Any memory tricks?

Fill in the missing vowels and consonants: p__c__l__ __r,   __e__u__ia__

Spelling rules

Add -**ly**: peculiar**ly**

→ Do some word art.   → Write a sentence with these words.

→ **1:1:1 doubling up preparation**

1. What do these mean? Have a guess.

→ Vowel and consonant suffixes

→ Syllables

→ Syllable stress

👍 It's perfectly OK if you don't know. We're going to look at these next.

The Doubling Up Rules — When and Why

Revision of key terms you need for this rule

➔ Suffixes are little words we add to the end of words:
   consonant suffixes: *-s, -ment, -ful, -ly, -ness...*
   vowel suffixes: *-ing, -ed, -er, -ant, -ance, -ent, -able, -ible...* And **-y** at the end of words.

➔ **Syllables** are little spoken chunks with a vowel or vowel sound in it.
   Read these out loud and slowly: *mum* ("mum"), *happy* ("hap-py"), *unhappy* ("un-hap-py").

   Breaking a word into syllables means:
   - you break a word down slowly into little spoken chunks,
   - each chunk is called a syllable,
   - each chunk usually has a vowel or vowel sound in it.

   1 syllable: *mum* — "mum"
   2 syllables: *happy* — "hap-py"
   3 syllables: *unhappy* — "un-hap-py"
   4 syllables: *particular* — "par-tic-u-lar"
   5 syllables: examination —"ex-am-in-a-tion"

👍 Breaking a word down into syllables can help you spell a word and remember the prefixes, suffixes and silent letters: "Wed-nes-day", "dis-ap-pear", "Feb-ru-a-ry".

➔ **Syllable stress**: When we say words, certain syllables can be stronger than others. Say the following words out loud and notice this: *careful, unhappy, begin, forget, prefer*
   First syllable stress: "CARE-ful"
   Second syllable stress: "un-HAP-py"
   Last syllable stress, which is important to remember when doubling up longer words:
   begin ("be-GIN"), *forget* ("for-GET"), occur ("oc-CUR")... *beginner, forgetting, occurrence*

➔ Important: Don't worry if syllables and stress are hard for you to hear or figure out; it's no problem. Find words within words to help or spot the vowels.

➔ **1:1:1 doubling up rule preparation**
➔ Do you know when and why we double up the consonant in these "little" words?
      put — putting, big — bigger, sun — sunny, swim — swimmer, shop — shopped

👍 It's perfectly OK if you don't know. We're going to discover this rule next.

1:1:1 Doubling Up Rule for Little Words

→ **When?**   We double up the end consonant with vowel suffixes

big — bigger, sun — sunny, quit — quitting, blur — blurred

→ **when** we have

1 syllable + **1** vowel next to **1** end consonant

hop

1:1:1

→ **Why?** The double letters indicate a short vowel sound, so we don't get the word mixed up with the magic 'e' silent 'e' long sound.

long: *hope — hoping*   short: *hop — hopping*

→ Say these words out loud and notice the short and long vowel sounds.

→ We never double up **w**, **x**, **y**, or **c**.

---

run — running, runny (but not **runs** — only double up with vowel suffixes)

thin — thinner, thinnest, thinned

swim — swimmer, swimming

sit — sitting, sitter, babysitter, babysitting

set — setting, settings, setting-up, setter, settle

big — bigger, biggest, biggish, biggie

sad — sadder, saddest, sadden, saddened

mad — madder, maddest, madden, maddening

stop — stopper, stopped, stopping, stoppage, unstoppable

slop — slopped, slopping, sloppy, sloppier, sloppiest

fat — fatter, fattest, fatten, fatting, fatty

hot — hotter, hottest

kid — kiddo, kiddie/kiddy, kidding, kidded

sun — sunned, sunning, sunny, sunnier, sunniest

blur — blurred, blurring, blurry

quiz — quizzing, quizzed, quizzes, quizzer, quizzical

whiz — whizzes, whizzed, whizzing, whizzer

*****quit** — quitting, quitter   *****squat** — squatting, squatted, squatter

*'q' is always spelled with a 'u' in English words, so the 'u' is not classed as an extra vowel.

swimming

*It's very **sunny** so I'm going **swimming**.*

→ Can you remember why we double up the end consonant?

→ Look at the pairs of words below. When you read them, you should be able to hear the difference between the short and long vowel sounds.

(hope) hoping vs hopping (hop)
hoped vs hopped

(slime) sliming vs slimming (slim)
slimed vs slimmed

(tape) taping vs tapping (tap)
taped vs tapped

Exercise

Write the root word, vowel sound and rule:

Word	Root word	Long or short vowel sound	Rule
hoping	hope	long	Drop the 'e' with -ing.
hopping	hop	short	1:1:1 doubling up rule.
rating			
ratting			
taped			
tapped			
pining			
pinning			
slimed			
slimmed			
biter			
bitter			

Answers

Word	Root word	Long or short vowel sound	Rule
hoping	hope	long	Drop the 'e' with -ing.
hopping	hop	short	1:1:1 doubling up rule.
rating	rate	long	Drop the 'e' with -ing.
ratting	rat	short	1:1:1 doubling up rule.
taped	tape	long	Drop the 'e' with -ed.
tapped	tap	short	1:1:1 doubling up rule.
pining	pine	long	Drop the 'e' with -ing.
pinning	pin	short	1:1:1 doubling up rule.
slimed	slime	long	Drop the 'e' with -ed.
slimmed	slim	short	1:1:1 doubling up rule.
biter	bite	long	Drop the 'e' with -er.
bitter	bit	short	1:1:1 doubling up rule.

Write a sentence with some of these words.

_____

_____

_____

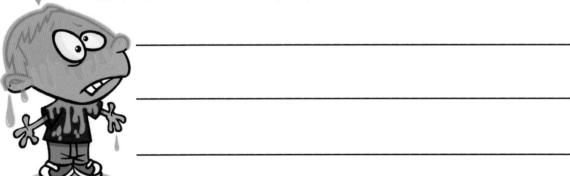

➔ We also double up longer words.
Do you know when we double up and when we don't?

begin — beginner, forget — forgetting, prefer — preferred, but not *preference*

It's perfectly OK if you don't know. We're going to discover this rule next.

1:1:1 Doubling Up Rule for Longer Words

→ We double up longer words if they end in

1 vowel + 1 end consonant and the **stress is on the end syllable***:

begin, forget prefer —"beGIN" "forGET" "preFER"

We only double up with vowel suffixes.

---

begin ("beGIN") – begi**nn**er, begi**nn**ing (not *begins* because 's' is not a vowel suffix)

forget ("forGET") – forge**tt**ing, forge**tt**able/unforge**tt**able

forgot — forgo**tt**en

regret — regre**tt**able, regre**tt**ably, regre**tt**ing, regre**tt**ed

upset — upse**tt**ing

forbid — forbi**dd**en, forbi**dd**ing

admit — admi**tt**ing, admi**tt**ance, admi**tt**ed, admi**tt**edly

commit — commi**tt**ed, commi**tt**ing, commi**tt**al, commi**tt**ee (not *commit**ment*** — consonant suffix)

submit — submi**tt**ing, submi**tt**ed

prefer — prefe**rr**ed, prefe**rr**ing (not ***preferable***, ***preference*** — stress on the first syllable)

When the stress isn't on the final syllable, don't double up:
gar**den** ("GARden") — *gardening, gardener*
lim**it** — *limiting, limited, limitation*

*If you can't hear the stress, no problem, see the spelling patterns or use a memory trick.

→ Remember to only double up with vowel suffixes. Compare these:
dropper/droplet, inner/inward, sunny/sunless, strappy/strapless, swimmer/swims
hottest/hotly, goddess/godly, shipping/shipment redden/redness

→ Remember with longer two syllable words, double up with a vowel suffix when the stress is on the last syllable. No doubling up with consonant suffixes.

pre**ferr**ed but preference   commi**tt**ed but commitment (consonant suffix)

  referring but referee   equi**pp**ed but equipment (consonant suffix)

                                          begi**nn**er but begins (consonant suffix)

Exercise

To double or not to double

Add the suffixes to these root words and double up or not:

Root word	Add -s	Add -ing	Add -ed (or is it an irregular past?)	Add -er, -ment or -ful if possible
stop	stops	stopping	stopped	stopper
swim			( )	
squat				
admit				———————
commit				
regret				
begin			( )	
prefer				———————
quiz				

➔ Remember, we double up longer words:
  • with vowel suffixes,
  • when the stress is on the last syllable.

➔ If you can't hear the stress, no problem, see the spelling patterns or use a memory trick.

VALLEY OF FORGOTTEN PASSWORDS

64

Exercice

To double or not to double

Root word	Add -s	Add -ing	Add -ed (irregular)	Add -er, -ment or -ful if possible
stop	stops	stopping	stopped	stopper
swim	swims	swimming	(swam)	swimmer
squat	squats	squatting	squatted	squatter
admit	admits	admitting	admitted	_____
commit	commits	committing	committed	commitment
regret	regrets	regretting	regretted	regretful
begin	begins	beginning	(began)	beginner
prefer	prefers	preferring	preferred	_____
quiz	quizzes*	quizzing	quizzed	quizzer

Adding -es to words

*We add **es** to words ending in **s, ss, z, x, ch, sh** to make plurals and third person singular for verbs: *He washes the dishes* and *she watches the TV. It crashes all the time.*
Plural nouns: *She has two businesses selling paint **brushes**.*

➔**es** is a vowel suffix so we can use the doubling up rule:
quiz — quizzes, whiz — whizzes have two rules: the 1:1:1 doubling up rule and adding -es rule.

gas — gases	wash — washes	bench — benches	fox — foxes	quiz — quizzes
class — classes	wish — wishes	church — churches	box — boxes	fizz — fizzes
gloss — glosses	bash — bashes	beach — beaches	fix — fixes	waltz — waltzes
prefix — prefixes	suffix — suffixes			

*key words ➔ **address** — address**es**, **business** — businesses, **possess** — possesses

➔Do some *word art* for addresses, businesses and possesses. ➔Write a sentence.

Exercise

Which is correct? Use the 1:1:1 rule or can you see what looks right?

Writing the root word might help.

1. ~~a. shoper~~ (b. shopper) <u>shop</u>

2. a. foxes b. foxxes _____

3. a. beginner b. beginer _____

4. a. fatest b. fattest _____

5. a. sleeping b. sleepping _____

6. a. forgetable b. forgettable _____

7. a. quicker b. quickker _____

8. a. budgetting b. budgeting _____

9. a. quized b. quizzed _____

10. a. appearing b. appearring _____

Remember, spelling only improves if you:

➤ study it
➤ practise it
➤ think about it
➤ notice it
➤ write it

Word Search

Words can go forwards, backwards, diagonally, vertically or horizontally! It's a hard one.

admittance
babysitter
beginner
committee
forbidden
forgotten
preferred
quitter
quizzing
shopping
sunnier
swimming
unforgettable
unstoppable
upsetting

```
d b i n v s m r j s f s e w e
g c a m e u w a e o m e q l d
v s e b i t l i r t t m b f e
b v e y y i t b m t t a n r r
u s v b d s i o i m t i r v r
a h m v x d i m g t i i u o e
d o a e d l m t e r w n s q f
m p o e x o u g t d o a g a e
i p n r c j r v x e r f v r r
t i z e o o q s p a r y h v p
t n o i f g n i t t e s p u u
a g u n s t o p p a b l e q l
n d u n g n i z z i u q d l n
c l u u z b e g i n n e r t m
e q b s w h e u b e i x b a j
```

Answers

1. (shop) ~~a. shoper~~ b. shopper (1:1:1 doubling up rule.)

2. (fox) a. foxes ~~b. foxxes~~ (Add **-es** to 'x' rule — never double up 'x'.)

3. (begin) a. beginner ~~b. beginer~~ (1:1:1 doubling up rule.)

4. (fat) ~~a. fatest~~ b. fattest (1:1:1 doubling up rule.)

5. (sleep) a. sleeping ~~b. sleepping~~ (2 vowels before final consonant so 'p' not doubled.)

6. (forget) ~~a. forgetable~~ b. forgettable (1:1:1 doubling up rule.)

7. (quick) a. quicker ~~b. quickker~~ (2 consonants at the end so 'k' not doubled.)

8. (budget) ~~a. budgetting~~ b. budgeting (Stress is on the "bud" so 't' not doubled.)

9. (quiz) ~~a. quized~~ b. quizzed (1:1:1 doubling up rule.)

10. (appear) a. appearing ~~b. appearring~~ (2 vowels before end consonant so don't double up.)

➔ -tion, -sion, -cian preparation

      mention, position, question, occasion, possession, electrician

➔ Why do we spell these "shun" sound endings like this when one spelling would do?

-tion, -sion, -cian

Key words: **mention, position, question, occasion, possession**

After his sensational television show, everyone wanted to question the magician about his new magical invention.

➔ Underline the -ation, -tion, -sion and -cian patterns.

➔These "shun" (-tion, -sion, -cian) suffix endings turn verbs into **nouns**.

➔They sound the same, or slightly similar, which can cause problems spelling them.

➔**-tion** is the most common ending.

➔**Answers**

The History Bit

We have these endings because most of them come from Latin. If the original Latin word ended in -t, -s or -c, then it was used in the English "shun" word.

mathematician from Latin *mathematicus*

invention from Latin *inventio(n)*

pension from Latin *pensio(n)*

passion from Latin *passio(n)*

The people who wrote the first dictionaries didn't care whether we could spell words easily, they just cared about the Latin origins of the word.

➔We have some rules to help us figure out which ending to use — some are easy to spot.

➔Look at these. Can you see the rules?

invent — inven**tion**

direct — direc**tion**

complete — comple**tion**

possess — posses**sion**

revise — revi**sion**

expand — expan**sion**, decide — deci**sion**

permit — permis**sion**

electric — electri**cian**

Read on to find out if you're right. It's perfectly OK if you don't know.

-tion

Congratulations on winning the **competition**!

After all the **emotion, preparation, action** and **perspiration**, we won.

➔Underline the -tion, -ation, -ition patterns.

-tion

1. When words end in **t**, add **ion** (-tion):

quest — ques**tion**	invent — invention	interrupt — interruption
suggest — sugges**tion**	prevent — prevention	erupt — eruption
insert — insertion	digest — digestion	exhibit — exhibition

2. When words end in **ct**, add **ion** (-ction):

act — ac**tion**	reject — rejection	protect — protection
react — reaction	inject — injection	direct — direction
collect — collection	inspect — inspection	correct — correction
select — selection	product — production	subtract — subtraction
elect — election	instruct — instruction	contract — contraction
extinct — extinction		

Also, *fiction, fraction*

3. When words end in **te, drop the 'e'** and add **ion** (-tion):

opposite — opposi**tion**	complete — comple**tion**
devote — devotion	pollute — poll**ution**
hibernate — hibernation	emote — emotion

-tion words without a rule: *mention, condition, attention, solution, caution, reception*

-ation

Adding -**ation** to a verb changes it into a noun.

1. Add -ation to make the pronunciation easier:

      present — presentation   *confront — confrontation*

      consult — consultation   *tempt — temptation*

      inform — information   *consider — consideration*

2. -ate ➜ -ation

   Change -**ate** to -**ation** (or drop the 'e' and add ion):

educate — education	*congratulate — congratulations*	*separate — separation*
locate — location	*populate — population*	*hesitate — hesitation*
inflate — inflation	*relate — relation*	*decorate — decoration*
frustrate — frustration	*create — creation*	*generate — generation*
operate — operation	*calculate — calculation*	*navigate — navigation*

3. Drop the 'e' and add **ation** in these words (-**ation**):

    invite — invitation   *prepare — preparation*   *imagine — imagination*

The 'a' makes these -tion words easier to say. You can hear the "a" sound in -**ation**, which helps with spelling them.

inspire — inspiration	*sense — sensation*	*examine — examination*
perspire — perspiration	*explore — exploration*	*combine — combination*
adore — adoration	*admire — admiration*	*continue — continuation*

4. Change the 'y' to 'i' and add **cation** (-**ication**):

     apply — application   *qualify — qualification*

     multiply — multiplication   *identify — identification*

5. Change the 'y' to 'i' and add **ation** (-**iation**): *vary — variation*

-ition

Drop the 'e' and add **ition** in these words **(-ition)**:

pose — position   compete — competition   define — definition

The 'i' makes these -ition words easier to say. You can hear the /I/ sound in **-ition**, which helps with spelling them.

Exercises   (Use your knowledge of the rules and pronunciation to help.)

1. Change these verbs into their -tion nouns:

act — <u>action</u>   invent — _____

inject — _____   complete — _____

hesitate — _____   pose — _____

quest — _____   inform — _____

apply — _____   direct — _____

2. Write the verb root word of each word:

protection — <u>protect</u>   separation — _____

exploration — _____   multiplication — _____

suggestion — _____   education — _____

3. Make these key words into their -ation nouns:

consider — _____   continue — _____

imagine — _____   separate — _____

Look back over the lesson and check your spellings and rules.

-ation letter pattern word lists

-cation
education
application
identification
multiplication
qualification

-ration
ration
adoration
admiration
decoration
exploration
inspiration
perspiration
preparation
separation
consideration

-tation
confrontation
expectation
hesitation
invitation
presentation
rotation
temptation
quotation

-nation
nation
combination
examination
fascination
imagination
determination

-lation
population
inflation
congratulations

-gation
navigation
investigation

-mation
formation
information

-sation
sensation
realisation
organisation
fossilisation

Saying these slowly, breaking them into syllables, can help you spell these: "in-for-ma-tion", "mul-ti-pli-ca-tion", "ex-plo-ra-tion".

Exercise

Change these verbs to their **-ation** nouns:

verbs ➔ nouns

examine ➔ <u>examination</u>

sense ➔ _____   admire ➔ _____

prepare ➔ _____   adore ➔ _____

inform ➔ _____   organise ➔ _____

image ➔ _____   consider ➔ _____

multiply ➔ _____   hesitate ➔ _____

apply ➔ _____   separate ➔ _____

Check your spellings against the words above.

1. Fill in the gaps with a consonant + a. Use colour if you want.

For example, presen__ __tion ➜ presen<u>ta</u>tion

infor__ __tion

ado__ __tion

sen__ __tion

prepa__ __tion

admi__ __tion

conside__ __tion

imagi__ __tion

sepa__ __tion

popu__ __tion

2. Check your spellings against the lists on the previous page.

3. Do some *word art.*

Key words
Which is correct?

1. a. question
   b. quesstion

2. a. position
   b. possition

3. a. mention
   b. menttion

question — *To go on a quest is to seek an answer to a question.*

question, questions, questioning, questioner, questionnaire, questionable

➜Do you have any memory tricks for this word?

➜Do some *word art* for *question*.

Fill in the missing letters:

q__ __st__ __n,   ques__ __ __ __,   __ue__ __io__,   _____

➜Write a sentence using this word.

_____

position — *He positioned himself on his scooter and posed.*

Drop the 'e' and add -ition: pose ➜ position

position, positioned, positions, positioning

➜Do you have any memory tricks?

Remember the word-within-a-word trick — po**s**ition.

See the vowels — p**o**s**i**t**i**o**n.

➜Do some *word art*.

Fill in the missing letters:

p__s__t__ __n,   po__ __ __ion,   __o__i__io__,   _____

➜Write a sentence using this word.

_____

mention

men + tion = mention

mention, mentioning, mentioned, mentions, unmentionable

➔ Do some *word art.*

Fill in the missing letters:

m__nt__ __n, __ __ __tion, men__ __ __ __, __e__ __io__, _____

➔ Write a sentence using this word.

_____

Do you now know which is correct?

1. a. possition
   b. position

2. a. question
   b. quesstion

3. a. menttion
   b. mention

➔ -sion preparation exercise

➔ Can you see how we form the -**sion** from the root word?

discuss — discussion, possess — possession

revise — revision, televise — television

decide — decision, explode — explosion

expand — expansion, extend — extension

permit — permission, admit — admission

-sion

Not as many nouns end in -**sion**.

Key words: **occasion, possession**

1. We often form -sion **nouns** from verbs ending in -**d**, -**de**, -**se**.

➔ Drop the end **de** or **d** and add -**sion**:

collide — collision   divide — division   suspend — suspension

decide — decision   explode — explosion   expand — expansion

erode — erosion   invade — invasion   comprehend — comprehension

conclude — conclusion   intrude — intrusion   extend — extension

Exceptions: *attend — attention, intend — intention*

➔ When words end in -**se**, **drop the 'e'** and add **ion**:

revise — revision   tense — tension   confuse — confusion

televise — television   verse — version   fuse — fusion

Also: occasion, pension, mansion

-ssion

2. When words end in -**ss**, just add **ion** (-**ssion**):

discuss — discussion   confess — confession   obsess — obsession

profess — profession   possess — possession   express — expression

depress — depression   process — procession

Also: *mission, passion, session, aggression, percussion*

3. -**mit** to -**mission**

Change mit to mission: *admit - admission*

permit — permission   omit — omission   commit — commission

submit — submission   transmit — transmission

➔ You might not remember these rules but hopefully you'll recognise the patterns.

Exercise

Add -sion to these words. Can you remember the rules?

explode — _____

divide — _____

possess — _____

expand — _____

collide — _____

revise — _____

conclude — _____

discuss — _____

admit — _____

permit — _____

invade — _____

extend — _____

Check your spellings against the lists of words on the previous page.

Word study

occasion(ally)   occasion ➜ occasional ➜ occasionally

Occasionally I have colourful candyfloss and I sit and eat it.

                    occasion

➜Can you think of any memory tricks?

➜Do some *word art.*

➜ *Write a sentence.*

_____

Fill in the missing letters:

        o__ __asionally,   occa__ __ __ __ally,   __cc__s__ __n__lly

    o__ __a__io__a__ __ __,   occasion__ __ __ __,   _____

---

possession

possess + ion = possession (See all those s's po**ss**e**ss**ion.)

possess, possession, possessing, possesses, possessed

Her most prized **possession** was her splendid swashbuckling silver sword.

➜Can you think of any memory tricks?   *possession*

➜Do some *word art.*

➜Write a sentence.

_____

Fill in the missing letters:

  po__ __e__ __ion, p__ss__ss__ __n, __o__ __e__ __ io__,   _____

-cian

-cian endings usually mean occupation, profession, or job: *electrician, politician, magician*

Most of these are made out of words ending in **-c**, so we just add **ian** (-cian):

music — musician   magic — magician

electric — electrician   optic — optician

politic — politician   mathematic — mathematician

Also: beauty (change the y to i) — *beautician*

Exercise
Add the correct **-cian** word.

1. Someone who works with electricity is an _____.

2. *Dynamo* is a famous _____ who does amazing magic tricks.

6. They play musical instruments and are often in bands or orchestras — they're

   _____.

7. She loves maths and wants to be a _____.

8. Someone who works in politics and is a Member of Parliament (MP):

   _____.

9. This professional checks your eyes: _____.

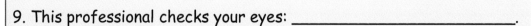

Answers

1. Someone who works with electricity is an **electrician**.

2. Dynamo is a famous **magician** who does amazing magic tricks.

6. They play musical instruments and are often in bands or orchestras — they're **musicians**.

7. She loves maths and wants to be a **mathematician**.

8. Someone who works in politics and is a Member of Parliament (MP): **politician**.

9. This professional checks your eyes: **optician**.

Exercise

Make these words into -tion, -sion, -ssion, or -cian nouns.

Use your knowledge of the rules, patterns, and pronunciation to help.

act	
examine	
electric	
inform	
magic	
discuss	
protect	
pose	
explode	
possess	

Answers

act	*action*
examine	*examination*
electric	*electrician*
inform	*information*
magic	*magician*
discuss	*discussion*
protect	*protection*
pose	*position*
explode	*explosion*
possess	*possession*

➔ Check your spellings carefully.

➔ Did the rules help you?

Did pronunciation help you for the 'ation' words?

Or did you see the letter patterns?

➔ What are the rules? Check below in the summary or go back over the previous pages to revise.

-tion, -sion, -cian summary

➔ Look at these. Can you remember the rules?

invent — invention, suggest — suggestion, invent — invention, opt — option

act — action, inject — injection, direct — direction, product — production

present — presentation, confront — confrontation, expect — expectation

complete — completion, devote — devotion, pollute — pollution, hibernate — hibernation

educate — education, hesitate — hesitation, create — creation

invite — invitation, inspire — inspiration, prepare — preparation

compete — competition, pose — position, define — definition

discuss — discussion, possess — possession

revise — revision, televise — television

decide — decision, explode — explosion

expand — expansion, extend — extension

permit — permission, admit — admission

electric — electrician, magic — magician, music — musician

➔ **-ous preparation exercise.** Which is correct?

1. a. various
   b. varyous

2. a. famous
   b. fameous

3. a. marvelous
   b. marvellous

4. a. glamorous
   b. glamourous

-ous

Key words: famous, various

We have *various, marvellous, adventurous* words in this section.

→ We add '**ous**' to nouns to make adjectives (describing words).

→ These 'ous' adjectives add more meaning than using *great, bad, good, nice, lovely.*

→ **-ous** is from Latin and means *full of, having to do with, all about, a quality:* *glorious* = full of glory, *joyous* = full of joy, *courageous* = full of courage.

Answers: 1. a. various 2. a. famous 3. b. marvellous (marvelous is the American spelling)
    4. a. glamorous

Spelling Rules:

1. **Add ous to root words** (complete words): *dangerous, poisonous, mountainous, joyous, marvel — marvellous* (double the 'l')

Sometimes, there's no obvious root word: *tremendous, enormous, jealous, fabulous, obvious serious, curious, previous*

2. **Change the end 'y' to 'i' when adding ous (-ious):** *vary – various*
   (You can hear the i/"ee" sound when you say these.)
   glory — glorious, fury — furious, mystery — mysterious

3. **Drop the 'e' when adding ous:** *fame — famous*
   nerve – nervous, adventure – adventurous, continue – continuous

4. **But keep the 'e' in these -ous words:** (You can hear the 'e' when you say these.)
   hideous, courteous, spontaneous

5. **Keep the 'e'** in these words to keep the soft 'g' sound (**-geous**):
   outrage — outrageous, courage — courageous, gorgeous

6. **Add –ly to make adverbs (-ously):**
   previously, seriously, nervously, cautiously, viciously, graciously, curiously, obviously

7. **Drop the 'u' in -our words when adding ous (-orous):** *glamour — glamorous, humour — humorous, vigour — vigorous*

Exercises

-ous is from Latin and means *full of, having to do with, all about.*

For example: She's *adventurous* and full of <u>adventure</u>.

1. It's *mountainous* so it's full of _____

2. They're *courageous* so they're full of _____

3. He's *humorous* so he's full of _____

4. It's *mysterious* so it's full of _____

5. *Famous* is all about _____

6. *Glamorous* is all about _____

Change these to their -ous adjective:

danger — _____   nerve — _____

vary — _____   humour — _____

courage — _____   fame — _____

poison — _____   glamour — _____

Put these -ous words in the gaps: *famous, nervous, various.*

He wants to be a _____ musician and play _____

types of music but he gets very _____ when he plays in

front of his friends.

Answers

1. It's *mountainous* so it's full of <u>mountains</u>.
2. They're *courageous* so they're full of <u>courage</u>.
3. He's *humorous* so he's full of <u>humour</u>.
4. It's *mysterious* so it's full of <u>mystery</u>.
5. *Famous* is all about <u>fame</u>.
6. *Glamorous* is all about <u>glamour</u>.

➔Now write a sentence like this for **nervous, poisonous** and **furious**.

_____

_____

_____

nerve — <u>nervous</u>	danger — <u>dangerous</u>
vary — <u>various</u>	humour — <u>humorous</u>
courage — <u>courageous</u>	fame — <u>famous</u>
poison — <u>poisonous</u>	glamour — <u>glamorous</u>

He wants to be a <u>famous</u> musician and play <u>various</u> types of music but
he gets very <u>nervous</u> when he plays in front of his friends.

➔Write a sentence like this with three of your favourite -ous words. Or write about these two.

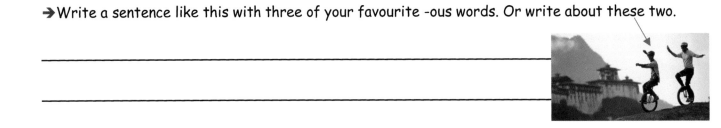

_____

_____

_____

_____

famous

Drop the 'e' with -ous: *fame* – *famous*

Fill in the missing letters: f__m__ __s,   fam__ __ __,   __a__ou__

→ Do some word art.

→ Write a sentence.

_____

_____

various

Change the 'y' to 'i' when adding -ous (-ious): *vary* – *various*

Fill in the missing letters: v__r__ __ __s,   vari__ __ __,   __a__iou__

→ Do some word art.

→ Write a sentence.

_____

_____

A Revision Exercise

Warning!

Multiple choice exercises can really mess with your brain because they give you spelling alternatives which also look right!

Multiple choice exercises are only useful when you can use various strategies to help you, such as:

- using memory tricks
- understanding spelling rules
- knowing common letter patterns
- seeing vowels

Look at these key words. Which is correct?

1. a. seperate
   b. separate

2. a. sentence
   b. sentance

3. a. different
   b. diferent

4. a. beleive
   b. believe

5. a. calender
   b. calendar

6. a. business
   b. buisness

7. a. peculier
   b. peculiar

8. a. address
   b. adress

9. a. possesion
   b. possession

10. a. naturally
    b. naturaly

11. a. experiance
    b. experience

12. a. accident
    b. accidant

13. a. favarite
    b. favourite

14. a. reguler
    b. regular

15. a. probabely
    b. probably

16. a. popular
    b. populer

17. a. famous
    b. fameous

18. a. disapear
    b. disappear

19. a. varyous
    b. various

20. a. diffacult
    b. difficult

21. a. purpose
    b. purpuse

22. a. grammer
    b. grammar

23. a. actualy
    b. actually

24. a. beginer
    b. beginner

25. a. position
    b. posistion

26. a. weight
    b. waight

27. a. presure
    b. pressure

Answers

1. a. ~~seperate~~
   b. separate

2. a. sentence
   b. ~~sentance~~

3. a. different
   b. ~~diferent~~

4. a. ~~beleive~~
   b. believe

5. a. ~~calender~~
   b. calendar

6. a. business
   b. ~~buisness~~

7. a. ~~peculier~~
   b. peculiar

8. a. address
   b. ~~adress~~

9. a. ~~possesion~~
   b. possession

10. a. naturally
    b. ~~naturaly~~

11. a. ~~experiance~~
    b. experience

12. a. accident
    b. ~~accidant~~

13. a. ~~favarite~~
    b. favourite

14. a. ~~reguler~~
    b. regular

15. a. ~~probabely~~
    b. probably

16. a. popular
    b. ~~populer~~

17. a. famous
    b. ~~fameous~~

18. a. ~~disapear~~
    b. disappear

19. a. ~~varyous~~
    b. various

20. a. ~~diffacult~~
    b. difficult

21. a. purpose
    b. ~~purpuse~~

22. a. ~~grammer~~
    b. grammar

23. a. ~~actualy~~
    b. actually

24. a. ~~beginer~~
    b. beginner

25. a. position
    b. ~~posistion~~

26. a. weight
    b. ~~waight~~

27. a. ~~presure~~
    b. pressure

➔ I know this type of exercise is not as hard as writing the word, so that's why it's important to use these words in a piece of writing, or get your friend to give you a spelling test, or write a story together. Or if you know the *Look, Say, Cover, Write, Check* method then use that, OK?

➔ What did you get wrong? A letter, the rule? By studying your mistakes, you can figure out how to remember the spelling next time. Don't forget to use memory tricks to help, and other spelling strategies you like.

These are the words I need to work on.

Remember, there are lots of ways to improve, learn and remember your spelling.

Just because you've seen a word once doesn't mean you're going to be able to spell it. You have to work on spelling and study it just like maths, art, history, or any other subject. To help, try to:

→ Understand the **meaning of the word** (use a dictionary).

→ Think of a **memory trick**, see **words within words**, or use **rhymes** and **sayings** to help spell the word.

→ Do word art — colour in the tricky bits and/or the vowels to help you see and remember.

→ Notice the **prefixes**, **suffixes**, and **spelling rules**.

→ Write a sentence and draw a picture.

→ Practise and work on your spelling constantly.

Go over this book again. Learning anything well takes a few goes, so keep going.

Congratulations – you're a star!

Give yourself a big pat on the back and a gold medal for finishing.

Keep on enjoying and loving spelling,
Joanne

A Bit About Me

I've been a teacher, lecturer and teacher trainer for 23 years and have written numerous books and online courses on spelling, punctuation and the history of spelling. I'm the owner of the spelling website, www.howtospell.co.uk.

My Books (available from Amazon)

For Kids

Spelling Rules and Patterns for Ages 10-11: To learn, improve & have fun with spelling and writing (for KS2 National Curriculum — years 5 and 6)

For Adults

Spelling Rules Workbook — a step-by-step guide to the rules of English spelling

Spelling Strategies & Secrets: the essential spelling guide

The Reasons Why English Spelling is so Weird and Wonderful

QTS Spelling Strategies (for trainee teachers)

Printed in Great Britain
by Amazon